Great American Stock Car Racing

Great American Stock Car Racing

by Angie Mayes

PREMIUM PRESS AMERICA

NASHVILLE, TENNESSEE

GREAT AMERICAN STOCK CAR RACING
by Angie Mayes

Copyright © 1997 by PREMIUM PRESS AMERICA

ISBN 1-887654-26-7

Library of Congress Catalog Card Number 97-66713

PREMIUM PRESS AMERICA books are available at special discounts for
premiums, sales promotions, fund-raising, or educational use. For details
contact the publisher at P.O. Box 159015, Nashville, TN 37215, or
phone (615) 256-8484, (800) 891-7323, or fax (615) 256-8624.

Cover by Bear Graves, Motorsports Graphics Ltd.
Edited by Melissa A. Chronister
Layout by Brent Baldwin

Printed by Dickinson Press Inc.

July 1997
1 2 3 4 5 6 7 8 9 10

Acknowledgements

Thanks to the following for their help and information which made this book a reality:

Marsha Ragland, Jack Ragland, Wendy Pearl, Emily Pearl (born during the Daytona 500!), Ginger Gosney, Nancy Houge, Jon Houge, Penny Copen, www.NASCAR.com (the most invaluable source), Winston Cup Scene, Circle Track Magazine, NASCAR Winston Cup Series Media Guide, Pro Set Racing Cards, MAXX Race Cards, NASCAR Preview and Press Guide, "American Zoom," Stock Car Racing Magazine.

Special thanks to my husband, Wes, for his patience and ability to answer most of the questions in this book; to Rick Houston of Winston Cup Scene for his support and encouragement in my pursuit of a career in racing; and to Richard Courtney for introducing me to George and Bette Schnitzer, without whom this book would not be possible.

Introduction

Start your engines and prepare to race through hundreds of surprising secrets behind America's hottest sport. Fasten your seatbelts for this crash course in stock car racing trivia. Angie steers you through the Winston Cup, Busch Grand National, Craftsman Truck Series, and much more.

GREAT AMERICAN STOCK CAR RACING is a true winner with any race fan, highlighting NASCAR greats such as Bobby Allison, Buck Baker, Ned Jarrett, Richard Petty, Cale Yarborough, and others. Every page reveals hobbies, nicknames, wrecks, and other fast facts that make these heroes one-of-a-kind. You'll discover a wide variety of new surprises, including early racing history and up-to-date records of current drivers.

From the starting line to the checkered flag, all the answers are included, so quiz yourself or quiz a friend. See how well you know your favorites—see if you belong in victory lane!

TABLE OF CONTENTS

Great American Stock Car Racing

NASCAR AND MUSIC CITY

1. Name the first racing-related country music album.

2. Columbia Records produced two NASCAR albums. One was "Hotter Than Asphalt." Name the other.

3. This country artist competed in 43 Grand National races in the 1960's and 1970's.

4. The first driver that drove Diamond Rio's Winston Cup car was _____.

5. Geoff Bodine and Darrell Waltrip sang on a country album. True or False?

6. Which country artist sang the theme for the stock car movie *Stroker Ace*?

7. Whose salsa company was a sponsor on Geoff Bodine's car?

8. Which country artist held the amateur track record at Nastrack driving school?

9. Which country group's song and video was called "Richard Petty Fans"?

10. Winston Cup cars used to visit what is now Nashville Speedway USA. True or False?

11. Which country duo hosts a Legends Car Series in Nashville each summer?

12. Which current driver "dabbled" in country music?

13. Kyle Petty sang a song about his dad entitled what?

14. A radio show dedicated to racing and country music is called what?

15. Which record company executive owned Richard Petty's race car in 1984?

NASCAR AND MUSIC CITY

ANSWERS

1. "NASCAR Goes Country"
2. "Running Wide Open"
3. Marty Robbins
4. Jay Hedgecock
5. True
6. Charlie Daniels
7. Tanya Tucker
8. T. Graham Brown
9. Alabama
10. True
11. Brooks & Dunn
12. Kyle Petty
13. "Oh, King Richard"
14. NASCAR Country
15. Mike Curb of Curb Records

SUPERSPEEDWAYS

1. All of this driver's wins at Michigan were back to back.

2. This driver left his car mid-race at the Talladega 500 in 1973 because "something" told him to quit.

3. What two new Winston Cup superspeedways opened in 1997?

4. This 44-acre lake has been the resting place for many drivers at Daytona International Speedway, including Goody's Dash Series driver Dave Stacy.

5. Which track saw the closest 1-2-3 race in history?

6. What was the first pace car at Daytona in 1959?

7. Who established the world's closed course speed record (221.120 m.p.h.) at Talladega in 1975?

8. The world closed course automotive race record (195.865 m.p.h.) is shared by these two current Winston Cup drivers. It was recorded in 1985 and again in 1986 at the Daytona 500.

9. Which driver has the most wins on superspeedways in a season?

10. Who is the oldest driver to win a race on a superspeedway?

11. Which current driver has the most consecutive wins on a superspeedway?

12. Which "modern day" driver has the most superspeedway wins (44)?

13. Since 1976, which superspeedway has hosted seven of the Top 11 competitive Winston Cup races, based on the number of lead changes (75)?

14. This tri-oval track in Pennsylvania measures 2.5 miles.

15. Which driver has won the most superspeedway races?

SUPERSPEEDWAYS

ANSWERS

1. Cale Yarborough
2. Bobby Isaac
3. California Speedway, Texas International Raceway
4. Lake Lloyd
5. Talladega
6. Bonneville Convertible
7. Mark Donohue
8. Terry Labonte ('85) and Dale Earnhardt ('86)
9. Bill Elliot ('85)
10. Harry Gant ('92 — 52 years old)
11. Bill Elliot (four)
12. David Pearson ('72-'86)
13. Talladega
14. Pocono
15. Richard Petty ('58-'92)

DAYTONA 500

1. No one has ever won the Daytona 500 and the
   _____ in the same year.

2. Which drivers won the Daytona 500 back to back?

3. Name the years that Richard Petty won this honor
   back to back.

4. The Daytona 500 trophy is also known as the
   _____ trophy.

5. For the second time in his career, _____
   held off Dale Earnhardt for the Daytona 500 win
   in 1996.

6. The winner of the 1963 Daytona 500 was

   _____.

7. What Winston Cup driver won the race with a checkerboard design on his car?

8. Who won the Daytona 500 four times ('68, '77, '83, '84)?

9. What current driver holds the Daytona 500 qualifying record?

10. Which regular Indy-car drivers also won the Daytona 500?

11. Who won the first Daytona 500?

12. Fireball Roberts ('62), Cale Yarborough ('68 and '84), Richard Petty ('66), Bill Elliot ('85 and '87) and _____ are the only drivers to win the Daytona 500 from the pole.

13. Which driver was the only one to win a "triple" award at Daytona (three races during speed weeks)?

14. He was the first to win the Daytona 500 and the Firecracker 250 in the same year.

15. Which two men, sharing the same last name, won the 1968 and 1969 Daytona 500 races, respectively?

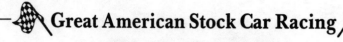

DAYTONA 500

ANSWERS

1. Winston Cup Championship
2. Cale Yarborough, Richard Petty and Sterling Marlin
3. 1973 and 1974
4. Harley J. Earl
5. Dale Jarrett
6. Tiny Lund
7. Derrick Cope in a Puralator car
8. Cale Yarborough
9. Bill Elliot (210.364 m.p.h.)
10. Mario Andretti ('67) and A.J. Foyt ('72)
11. Lee Petty
12. Buddy Baker ('80)
13. Cale Yarborough
14. Fireball Roberts ('62)
15. Cale (1968) and Lee Roy (1969) Yarborough

WINNING

1. He has won a race every year since he started in 1983.

2. In 1996, Bobby Hamilton brought a Petty enterprises-owned car to victory lane for the first time since what year?

3. In Richard Petty's last two wins (#199, 200) in 1984, the car was owned by whom?

4. The late Elmo Langley ended his NASCAR racing career in _____, nearly 15 years after winning his first and second (and only) races.

5. To win the Winston Million, a driver has to win what races at what tracks?

13

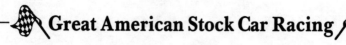

6. What uncredited driver led an actual race at Phoenix International Raceway in a Rich Hendrick Research and Development (R&D) car in the movie "Days of Thunder"?

7. Which driver has won more money than any other driver?

8. No defending champion of the Winston Select 500 has repeated as the winner since _____ in 1975 and 1976, breaking David Pearson's string of three wins, 1972-74.

9. Who took a stunning win at Talladega in 1988 with Andy Petree as his crew chief?

10. Who was the youngest driver to ever win a race?

Great American Stock Car Racing

11. Name the modern day driver with the most wins in a season.

12. Which modern day driver has won the most races from the pole?

13. Which modern day driver has dominated the short tracks with the most wins in his career?

14. Which year saw the most first time winners?

15. Which set of brothers has four wins—two each—in 1995?

Great American Stock Car Racing

WINNING

ANSWERS

1. Ricky Rudd
2. 1983
3. Mike Curb
4. 1966
5. Daytona 500, Daytona; Winston Select 500, Talladega; Coca Cola 600, Charlotte; Southern 500, Darlington
6. Bobby Hamilton
7. Dale Earnhardt
8. Buddy Baker
9. Phil Parsons
10. Donald Thomas
11. Richard Petty with 13 in 1975
12. Darrell Waltrip (24)
13. Darrell Waltrip (17)
14. 1988
15. Terry and Bobby Labonte

THE WINSTON

1. Which younger brother of a former Winston Cup champion staged a major upset at the 1996 Winston?

2. Who won the first Winston?

3. The Winston is the richest race per _____ in all of motorsports.

4. The race was to be run on various tracks, the second being _____. They now hold the race at Charlotte each year.

5. The race is sponsored by _____.

6. Which current driver has won the most Winston events?

7. To get into the Winston, a driver must have won races in the _____ years.

8. The race is run in _____ segments.

9. Who won each of the segments in 1995?

10. The first Winston was held in what year?

11. There are special entrance exceptions: one for a champion who is still an active driver and another for the past five winners of the _____.

12. The winner of the Winston Open is not guaranteed a spot in the Winston Select. True or False?

13. All Winston Cup competitors are invited to compete in the Winston Open. True or False?

14. Dale Earnhardt changed his car color to
    _____ in 1995 to commemorate R.J.
    Reynolds' 25th anniversary.

15. The Winston Select has at least _____ cars
    in the field.

THE WINSTON

ANSWERS

1. Michael Waltrip
2. Darrell Waltrip
3. Mile
4. Atlanta
5. R.J. Reynolds
6. Darrell Waltrip
7. Preceding and current
8. Three
9. Jeff Gordon
10. 1985
11. Winston Select
12. False
13. True
14. Silver
15. 20

Great American Stock Car Racing

NASCAR AND THE FANS

1. Gaylord Entertainment and NASCAR have a chain of theme stores called what?

2. What is the official destination of NASCAR?

3. An interactive mini-theme park at Daytona is called what?

4. _____ is just one of many restaurants with stock car themes. The first one opened in Myrtle Beach.

5. NASCAR has an online address. True or False?

6. TNN hosts an event for racing enthusiasts each summer at Opryland. It is called _____.

7. Each year the fans vote on an award given at the Winston Cup awards banquet. What is it called?

8. As of 1996, which driver has been voted a fan favorite 11 times?

9. Who broke Elliot's string of wins?

10. Who was the first driver to win the favorite driver award?

11. When the race was stopped early because the track's surface "came up," nearly 10,000 fans held drivers and teams hostage in 1961 at the Asheville-Weaverville (NC) Speedway. True or False?

12. NASCAR drivers usually charge for autographs. True or False?

13. Jeff Gordon and Richard Petty are part-owners in this Orlando, Florida-based restaurant.

14. This company made the first race cards; they were similar to baseball cards and have become very popular since their debut in 1988.

15. This organization sponsored the NASCAR Family Cruise, a fan-based cruise which featured many NASCAR drivers.

NASCAR AND THE FANS

ANSWERS

1. NASCAR Thunder
2. Opryland USA
3. Daytona USA
4. NASCAR Cafe
5. True (www.NASCAR.com)
6. Salute To Motorsports
7. "Most Popular Driver" award
8. Bill Elliot
9. Darrell Waltrip
10. Lee Petty
11. True
12. False
13. Race Rock
14. Maxx Race Cards
15. Winston Cup Racing Wives Auxiliary

CREW CHIEFS

1. Which former crew chief rejoined Darrell Waltrip in 1996?

2. Who has been the Petty Enterprises crew chief since 1991, helping Bobby Hamilton capture his first win?

3. His call helped Jeff Gordon capture his first win in 1994.

4. This former Davey Allison crew chief switched to Dale Earnhardt's team for the 1997 season.

5. This Bobby Labonte crew chief is Dale Jarrett's brother-in-law (and former crew chief).

6. This man helped revitalize Terry Labonte's career and helped guide him to a 1996 championship.

7. Which crew chief is the son of a legendary crew chief and helped guide Dale Jarrett to a successful 1996 season?

8. He used to build stock cars for Bobby Hamilton at Nashville (TN) International Raceway.

9. He was Rusty Wallace's crew chief for the 1989 Championship, later moving to Kyle Petty's team and then to the Craftsman Truck Series.

10. Who was the crew chief for Sterling Marlin's 1994 and 1995 Daytona 500 wins?

11. He left Dale Earnhardt's team to become part-owner in Leo Jackson's #33 team.

12. This crew chief built engines that won three Daytona 500's.

13. Who used to be the crew chief for his brother-in-law, Brett Bodine?

14. He worked with Alan Kulwicki as crew chief before his death.

15. This Winston Cup driver wants to be a crew chief when he retires.

CREW CHIEFS

ANSWERS

1. Jeff Hammond
2. Robbie Loomis
3. Ray Evernham
4. Larry McReynolds
5. Jimmy Makar
6. Gary DeHart
7. Todd Parrott
8. Gil Martin
9. Barry Dodson
10. Tony Glover
11. Andy Petree
12. Waddell Wilson
13. Donnie Richardson
14. Paul Andrews
15. Ted Musgrave

TRACKS

1. At what track did this happen? Cale Yarborough and Sam McQuagg were in a battle for the lead when the two cars touched and Cale went over the wall and landed in the parking lot.

2. The first race at this track, the World 600, took 5 hours and 34 minutes to complete.

3. The last race at this Winston Cup track took place in 1996.

4. When was the last convertible race at Darlington?

5. Both qualifying races were canceled at Daytona in 1968 because of what?

6. "Fireball" Roberts, Cale Yarborough and Bill Elliot are the only three drivers to score a "slam" at the Daytona 500. What is a "slam"?

7. What are the two road courses in Winston Cup competition?

8. What is the longest track in Winston Cup competition?

9. Which track hosts the night race in August?

10. At this track you get "the stripe," especially when you hit its famed 23-25 degree turns.

11. What headache powder sponsors this race at Martinsville?

12. Hosting a Winston Cup race since 1969, the second yearly race at this track used to be called the "Yankee 500."

13. Ricky Rudd has shown his prowess at road racing at this California track by winning four poles since 1990.

14. Darrell Waltrip can claim the most consecutive wins (7) at this Tennessee track from 1981-84.

15. This track now hosts the Winston Select event each May.

Great American Stock Car Racing

TRACKS

ANSWERS

1. Darlington
2. Charlotte Motor Speedway
3. North Wilkesboro
4. 1962 (Rebel 300)
5. Rain
6. Pole, fast qualifier and winner
7. Sears Point and Watkins Glen
8. Talladega (2.66 miles, Daytona is 2.5 miles long)
9. Bristol
10. Darlington
11. Goody's
12. Michigan
13. Sears Point
14. Bristol
15. Charlotte

Great American Stock Car Racing

ROOKIES

1. This 1977 Rookie of the Year took seven years to win his first race. He's won at least one every year afterwards.

2. This Rookie of the Year had no competition in 1996.

3. This champion ran for Rookie of the Year honors versus Dale Earnhardt, Harry Gant, and Joe Millikan.

4. He is the oldest driver to win Rookie of the Year.

5. This driver was a rookie when he won his first Winston Cup race in 1987.

6. Who won the 1979 Rookie of the Year and the 1980 Winston Cup championship?

7. Who was the first Rookie of the Year?

8. Bobby Hamilton won the 1991 Rookie of the Year title over what current driver?

9. Which one of these drivers was not a Rookie of the year in the 1980's: Geoff Bodine, Sterling Marlin, Rusty Wallace, Ken Schrader, Alan Kulwicki, Davey Allison, Dick Trickle, Bobby Labonte.

10. Which brothers were Rookie of the Year winners in 1981 and 1988, respectively?

Great American Stock Car Racing

11. Six Winston Cup Rookie of the Year titlists went on to win the Winston Cup Championship. They are Richard Petty, Dale Earnhardt, David Pearson, Rusty Wallace, Alan Kulwicki and _____.

12. The Rookie of the Year competition is sponsored by which race card company?

13. Which Rookie of the Year has a successful All Pro career?

14. The Rookie of the Year title is based on the 15 best _____ of the season.

15. Which 1992 Rookie of the Year candidate now races in the truck division?

ROOKIES

ANSWERS

1. Ricky Rudd
2. Johnny Benson
3. Terry Labonte
4. Dick Trickle (48 years old)
5. Davey Allison
6. Dale Earnhardt
7. Shorty Rollins
8. Ted Musgrave
9. Bobby Labonte
10. Ron and Ken Bouchard
11. Jeff Gordon
12. Maxx Race Cards
13. Jody Ridley
14. Finishes
15. Jimmy Hensley (1992 winner)

Great American Stock Car Racing

RECORDS

1. He broke Richard Petty's string of consecutive starts (513) in April 1996 at Martinsville.

2. Dale Earnhardt and Richard Petty have tied for this number of championships.

3. Which legendary car owner has a record of 609 consecutive starts?

4. Who is the winningist active driver at Daytona?

5. This driver has the most poles (11) at one track (Charlotte) since 1949.

6. Which late driver has the most poles for a season?

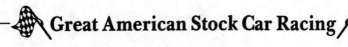

7. From 1972 to 1995, this driver from Owensboro, Kentucky, had 59 poles.

8. Which driver has started the most races in his career (1,177)?

9. Which driver made the most money in one season, including championship money?

10. This driver has won the most bonus money ($1,000,000).

11. Which active driver has won the most races from the pole?

12. Which late driver started the most consecutive races without a single win (653)?

Great American Stock Car Racing

13. This driver has the best win percentage for his career: 40 wins, 189 starts, 1949-1961.

14. Which driver — the father of a current Busch Grand National driver — won 11 races in 18 starts in 1973?

15. Which driver raced more than 200 m.p.h. 15 times during his career?

RECORDS

ANSWERS

1. Terry Labonte
2. Seven
3. Bud Moore
4. Dale Earnhardt
5. David Pearson
6. Bobby Isaac (20 in 1969)
7. Darrell Waltrip
8. Richard Petty
9. Jeff Gordon
10. Bill Elliot
11. Darrell Waltrip (24 from '72-'95)
12. J.D. McDuffie
13. Tim Flock, 21.2 percent
14. David Pearson
15. Cale Yarborough

Great American Stock Car Racing

SECOND GENERATION DRIVERS

*Match these racing children with
their parental counterparts*

1.	Ned Jarrett	a.	Kelley
2.	Bobby Allison	b.	Adam
3.	Richard Petty	c.	Kyle
4.	Arlo Andretti	d.	Dale
5.	Dale Earnhardt	e.	Davey
6.	Geoff Bodine	f.	Glenn
7.	Dale Jarrett	g.	Richard
8.	Bill France	h.	Ricky
9.	Ralph Earnhardt	i.	Barry
10.	Bobby Hamilton	j.	Jason
11.	Kyle Petty	k.	John
12.	Lee Petty	l.	Bobby
13.	Rick Hendrick	m.	Brian

Great American Stock Car Racing

SECOND GENERATION DRIVERS

ANSWERS

1. f
2. e
3. c
4. k
5. a
6. i
7. j
8. m
9. d
10. l
11. b
12. g
13. h

Great American Stock Car Racing

1. Which college's logo was displayed on the #1 Winston Cup car?

2. Which Winston Cup driver has a degree in business management from Moravian (PA) College? (He was on the dean's list!)

3. Which Winston Cup driver has an associate's degree in mechanical engineering from the State University of New York at Alfred?

4. Which college has a program which incorporates race car engineering into its program?

5. The same college sends interns to work with race teams. True or False?

6. Wisconsin driver _____ received a mechanical engineering degree from the University of Wisconsin at Madison.

7. Which driver majored in mechanical engineering at the Florida Institute of Technology?

8. Jeff Gordon and Ray Evernham lectured at _____ University, making them the first NASCAR participants to lecture at an Ivy League school.

9. Which Winston Cup driver received a law degree from the University of Washington?

10. Which driver turned down a football grant from the University of Alabama?

11. This driver is a big fan of the University of Tennessee football team, often hanging out with players on the sideline during home games in Knoxville.

12. This driving school is considered the "granddaddy" of all stock car schools.

13. This ARCA champion is the director of the Fast Track High Performance Driving School.

14. This big man at Charlotte Motor Speedway went to the University of South Carolina on a football scholarship.

15. This Kodak car owner attended Richmond Professional University before "breaking" into Winston Cup.

SCHOOLS

ANSWERS

1. University of Nebraska
2. John Andretti
3. Brett Bodine
4. Clemson
5. True
6. Alan Kulwicki
7. Joe Nemechek
8. Princeton
9. Chad Little
10. Steve Grissom
11. Sterling Marlin
12. Buck Baker's Racing School
13. Andy Hillenburg
14. Humpy Wheeler
15. Larry McClure

Great American Stock Car Racing

NICKNAMES

*Match these drivers with
their nickname*

1. Neil Castles
2. Terry Labonte
3. Roy Jones
4. Fred Lorenzen
5. Jeff Gordon
6. David Pearson
7. Edwin Keith Matthews
8. Tom Pistone
9. Danny Myers
10. Jack Elders
11. Darrell Waltrip
12. Jack Ingram
13. Jimmy Spencer

a. Tiger
b. Silver Fox
c. Ironman
d. Jaws
e. Soapy
f. Suitcase
g. Buckshot
h. Mr. Excitement
i. Iceman
j. Fearless Freddy
k. Chocolate
l. Wonder Boy
m. Banjo

NICKNAMES

ANSWERS

1. e
2. i
3. g
4. j
5. l
6. b
7. m
8. a
9. k
10. f
11. d
12. c
13. h

Great American Stock Car Racing

EARLY RACING HISTORY

1. Automotive competition at Daytona Beach began in what year?

2. The final land speed record run on _____ was in 1935 (the event went to the Bonneville Salt Flats in Utah after that).

3. Daytona Beach was known as the birthplace of

   _____.

4. Stock car racing on the beach began in 1936 and lasted until this year.

5. The original track size was _____ miles.

6. Bill _____ , a local mechanic, entered the beach race in 1936.

7. The race stopped during WWII but resumed in what year? (Motorcycle racing resumed the following year.)

8. _____ , who had been promoting the beach race since 1938, founded NASCAR in 1948.

9. The International Sweepstakes, the first _____-mile race at the new Superspeedway, began in 1959.

10. The first winner of the International Sweepstakes event was _____, but three days later Lee Petty was named the winner (by just two feet).

11. The first "new car" race was held at this track in 1949.

12. Darlington was built in the late 1940's, and in 1950 the first _____ took place.

13. What year did Grand National drivers go on strike?

14. During WWII, _____ built submarine chasers.

15. The National Stock Car Racing Association, NASCRA, was the first suggestion for a name, but a small group in Georgia already had the name; therefore, driver-mechanic Red Vogt suggested the National Association For Stock Car Automobile Racing, NASCAR. True or False?

EARLY RACING HISTORY

ANSWERS

1. 1903
2. Daytona Beach
3. Speed
4. 1958
5. 3.2
6. France
7. 1946
8. Bill France, Sr.
9. 500
10. Johnny Beauchamp
11. Charlotte Motor Speedway
12. Southern 500
13. 1969
14. Bill France, Sr.
15. True

Great American Stock Car Racing

BUSCH GRAND NATIONAL

1. This family had three sons in Busch Grand National in 1996.

2. Bace Motorsports took the 1995 and 1996 BGN Championship with two different drivers. Name them.

3. Which BGN driver competed in the inaugural race in Japan in 1996?

4. Which 1991 BGN Rookie of the Year went on to take a Winston Cup championship?

5. Only three drivers have been the BGN champ twice. Who are they?

6. Only two BGN Rookies have won the championship. Name them.

7. At Rockingham, who won his last NASCAR and first BGN series race?

8. No BGN champion has ever won a Winston Cup championship. True or False?

9. Jimmy Spencer was a BGN regular in 1988 and again in what year?

10. Who won the first BGN event in 1982?

11. What was BGN initially called?

12. This Gadsen, Alabama, native was 22 years old when he won the All Pro series title. He took the BGN title at 30 years of age.

Great American Stock Car Racing

13. Which Winston Cup driver is extremely consistent in a BGN car?

14. Owensboro, Kentucky, has produced its share of top drivers, among them this 1995 BGN champion.

15. This female BGN regular formed her own team in 1996.

Great American Stock Car Racing

BUSCH GRAND NATIONAL

ANSWERS

1. The Green Family (David, Jeff and Mark) from Owensboro, Kentucky
2. Johnny Benson and Randy LaJoie
3. David Green
4. Jeff Gordon
5. Larry Pearson, Jack Ingram, Sam Arnd
6. Joe Nemechek and Johnny Benson
7. David Pearson
8. True
9. 1992
10. Dale Earnhardt
11. NASCAR Budweiser Late Model Sportsman Division
12. Steve Grissom
13. Mark Martin
14. David Green
15. Patty Moise

Great American Stock Car Racing

1. What soft drink sponsor in the movie *Days of Thunder* became an actual Winston Cup sponsor?

2. What political campaign "sponsored" the car of Robbie Faggart as he attempted to qualify for the 1996 Southern 500?

3. Which laundry detergent company was one of the first non-automotive-related sponsors in Winston Cup?

4. Which wrestling organization sponsored the #29 Busch Grand National car?

5. Scooby Doo and Fred Flintstone were part of whose sponsorship of the #29 Winston Cup car?

6. What official film of NASCAR also sponsors a car?

7. No matter what the type of beer — Lite, Genuine Draft — Rusty Wallace's main sponsor stays the same. What is it?

8. The sales of Goody's Headache Powders almost doubled once they became involved in stock car racing. True or False?

9. Which manufacturer pulled out of Busch Grand National/Winston Cup racing in the 1970's and stayed out until 1981?

10. Which sports drink company sponsored Darrell Waltrip?

11. The "Brake of the Race" award is sponsored by what company?

12. The "Mechanic of the Race" award is sponsored by what auto parts company?

13. Which company celebrated 25 years of sponsorship with Richard Petty in 1996?

14. The main sponsor for Winston Cup racing is what tobacco company?

15. What driver changed his color and sponsor for the inaugural race at Suzuka City in Japan?

Great American Stock Car Racing

SPONSORS

ANSWERS

1. Mello Yellow
2. Dole/Kemp '96
3. Tide
4. World Championship Wrestling (WCW)
5. Cartoon Network
6. Kodak
7. Miller
8. True
9. Ford
10. Gatorade
11. Raybestos
12. Western Auto
13. STP
14. R.J. Reynolds
15. Earnhardt (to A.C. Delco)

BUSCH CLASH

1. The winner of the first Busch Clash was what current-day TV announcer?

2. The Busch Clash is sponsored by what company?

3. Where is the Busch Clash run?

4. To qualify for the Clash, a driver must have won a pole for a race the prior year, or win the coin toss at the end of the season. True or False?

5. The race is run in two _____ lap segments. The winner of segment two takes the check.

6. Dale Earnhardt won the Busch Clash four times in the same year he won the championship. What other driver did the same (1981)?

7. This Pittsboro, Indiana, driver won the Busch Clash the first time he ran it.

8. What year did the Busch Clash begin?

9. What driver has won more Clashes than any other?

10. This driver won the 9th Clash in 1984 with car #9. Name him.

11. The Busch Grand National driver with the most poles is also allowed to compete in the Busch Clash. True or False?

12. A Winston Cup "wild card" entry is also included in the Clash. True or False?

Great American Stock Car Racing

13. The Busch Clash is run the week prior to what race?

14. The lineup for the second segment in the Clash is determined by doing what to the finishing order of the first segment?

15. The following have won the Clash but not the Winston Cup Championship: Buddy Baker, Neil Bonnett, Kenny Schrader and _____.

BUSCH CLASH

ANSWERS

1. Buddy Baker
2. Anheuser-Busch
3. Daytona International Speedway
4. False, the coin toss is not a part of the determination.
5. 10
6. Darrell Waltrip
7. Jeff Gordon
8. 1979
9. Dale Earnhardt
10. Bill Elliot
11. True
12. True
13. Daytona 500
14. Inverting
15. Geoff Bodine

Great American Stock Car Racing

TRUE OR FALSE

Answer true or false to each of the following:

1. Curtis Turner was suspended by NASCAR in 1961 for trying to unionize the drivers.

2. Bobby Hamilton won two poles in 1996 and therefore was in the Busch Clash.

3. The speedway stocks (on the stock market) are not offered to the general public.

4. When R.J. Reynolds initially put up the money for the first Winston Million, they didn't think anyone would win. Elliot surprised them.

5. The National Motorsports Press Association's Hall of Fame is located at Rockingham.

Great American Stock Car Racing

6. Dale Jarrett drove his first professional race at Hickory, North Carolina, in 1977 in a car built by Andy Petree and Jimmy Newsome.

7. Jim Boy and Bucky are a popular syndicated radio duo who love racing.

8. Bobby Labonte and Joe Gibbs Racing honor a different baseball team each race day by wearing a helmet with the team's logo emblazoned on it.

9. NASCAR opened an office in Washington, D.C., in 1996.

10. Speed Buggy joined forces with ESPN and NASCAR for a promotional campaign.

11. The Joe Weatherly Museum is at Darlington Raceway.

12. Richard Petty was the first inductee of the North Carolina Auto Racing Hall of Fame.

13. Harry Hogge built Rick Hendrick's first cars and also served as the team's crew chief.

14. Ken Schrader's first Winston Cup ride was for the late Elmo Langley.

15. Eli Gold also announces football games for Auburn University.

Great American Stock Car Racing

TRUE OR FALSE

ANSWERS

1. True
2. False (Petty Enterprises does not run the Busch Beer logo on the #43 car, so Hamilton and the team are not eligible for the Clash.)
3. False
4. True
5. False (Darlington)
6. True
7. False (John Boy and Billy are the duo, based out of Charlotte.)
8. False (The helmets are painted with FOOTBALL team logos.)
9. False (New York City)
10. False (It was Speed Racer.)
11. True
12. True
13. False (Harry Hyde was his name.)
14. True
15. False (University of Alabama)

Great American Stock Car Racing

HOBBIES

1. What driver from Chesapeake, Virginia, enjoys listening to Elton John music?

2. This third-generation driver loves riding his Harley Davidson motorcycle.

3. What former Daytona 500 winner is an excellent golfer?

4. This seven time Winston Cup champion driver loves to fish and hunt.

5. He's flown in a race car (he holds the fastest race speed record) and loves to fly in a plane.

6. This driver loves video games.

7. This two-time Daytona 500 winner loves to collect Civil War relics.

8. This Roush driver is a devout body builder.

9. This Wisconsin driver loves to restore vintage vehicles.

10. This Missouri native loves collecting old cars and trucks.

11. This driver loves roller skating.

12. Karaoke is the favorite hobby of this Alabama driver.

13. This driver, the youngest of three brothers, loves the St. Louis Cardinals.

14. His oldest brother loves the NHRA.

15. This driver "dabbles" with computers and remote control cars.

HOBBIES

ANSWERS

1. Ricky Rudd
2. Kyle Petty
3. Derrike Cope
4. Dale Earnhardt
5. Bill Elliott
6. Jeff Gordon
7. Sterling Marlin
8. Mark Martin
9. Ted Musgrave
10. Ken Schrader
11. Morgan Shepherd
12. Hut Stricklin
13. Kenny Wallace
14. Rusty Wallace
15. Bobby Labonte

COOL FACTS

1. Who started his first Winston Cup race as a 17-year-old high school student in 1982?

2. His grandfather built cars for the late country singer Marty Robbins.

3. He is A.J. Foyt's godson.

4. Richard Petty is a staunch Republican. He ran for what North Carolina office in 1996?

5. Bobby Hamilton won at Phoenix International Raceway, a track where he first caught Winston Cup's eye as a driver in what?

6. He traded $300 worth of lumber for a motor for his son Dale's first race car.

7. He and his family have a "dirt track" next to the family's auto parts business. Winston Cup drivers "race" there during Pocono weekends.

8. There are just six drivers who have made $1 million in two series (Busch Grand National and Winston Cup). They are Bobby Labonte, Robert Pressley, Kenny Wallace, Steve Grissom, Dale Jarrett and _____.

9. Which driver raced in the Indianapolis 500 and the Coca Cola 600 on the same day?

10. This driver and the Penske Racing team worked with Rockwell Space Systems Division in 1996.

11. The _____ season is where drivers, teams and sponsors switch around.

12. In the 1938 _____ beach race, lap winners were offered a bottle of rum, $2.50 credit at a local men's store, a box of fancy Hav-A-Tampa cigars, a case of Pennzoil oil and a $25 credit toward the purchase of a car at a local used automobile lot.

13. Bill Broderick, the Unocal 76 P.R. man seen in Victory Lane each week, is often referred to as the _____ because of the hats he gives the drivers to wear for various photos.

14. What racing publication as known as the bible of stock car racing?

15. This Winston Cup driver's dad, Vic, first invented the "war wagon" rolling tool box.

COOL FACTS

ANSWERS

1. Bobby Hillen
2. Bobby Hamilton
3. John Andretti
4. Secretary of State
5. *Days of Thunder*
6. Ned Jarrett
7. Jimmy Spencer
8. Mark Martin
9. John Andretti
10. Rusty Wallace
11. Silly
12. Daytona
13. Hat Man
14. *Winston Cup Scene*
15. Ernie Irvan

CAR OWNERS

1. Which two team owners have won back to back championships with different drivers?

2. As of 1997, Petty Enterprises has been in racing for _____ years.

3. The _____ Brothers have been together for 800 races over 45 years.

4. Dale Earnhardt has raced for how many Winston Cup car owners since 1975?

5. Junior Johnson left racing as car owner at the end of the ____ season.

6. Who moved his race team from Hueytown to Charlotte in 1996?

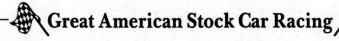

7. Chad Little's BGN car owner was which Washington Redskin football player?

8. Which car owner owns the second largest Hispanic-owned company in America?

9. He bought the team from the Alan Kulwicki estate.

10. This car owner has earned more prize money than any other in the history of Winston Cup.

11. Which car owner was formerly an NFL coach?

12. Which Winston Cup driver also has owned his car for over 30 years?

13. This triple team car owner is a former drag racer.

14. This team owner was one of the original members of the Mach One team owned by Burt Reynolds and Hal Needham during Harry Gant's Skoal Bandit career.

15. This "car owner" won 269 races from 1949 to 1996, with over 2,000 entries in nearly 1,650 races.

Great American Stock Car Racing

CAR OWNERS

ANSWERS

1. Carl Kiekhaefer and Rick Hendrick
2. 48 years
3. Wood
4. Nine
5. 1995
6. Bobby Allison
7. Mark Rypien
8. Felix Sabates
9. Geoff Bodine
10. Rick Hendrick
11. Joe Gibbs
12. Dave Marcis
13. Jack Roush
14. Travis Carter
15. Petty Enterprises

MONEY AND OTHER
IMPORTANT NUMBERS

1. If the Winston Million had been in effect, two other drivers would have won the money. Name them.

2. Richard Petty Enterprises celebrated his ___ year in racing in 1996 with commemorative colors on the #43 car.

3. He is only the third driver to hit the $15 million mark. He did it in 1996 with much fanfare.

4. Last place in the _____ Select pays $18,000.

5. First place in a race garners the driver how many points?

6. In a 44 car field, last place gets this number of points.

7. Leading a lap gives a driver _____ extra points.

8. This driver captured the sport's highest year-end paycheck to date: $4.3 million in 1995 (total season earnings).

9. There have been nearly _____ different Winston Cup winners (1949-1996).

10. The 1984 Winston 500 at _____ saw 75 lead changes in 188 laps.

11. This Winston Cup driver has won the most money (more than $28 million at the end of the 1996 season).

12. Jeff Gordon won a race high of $613,000 at the

    _____.

13. This driver led the most laps at the 1961 Daytona 500 but didn't win.

14. This driver is second to Richard Petty in wins and poles.

15. This Busch Grand National driver has won the most money in that division (more than $1.8 million).

Great American Stock Car Racing

MONEY AND OTHER IMPORTANT NUMBERS

ANSWERS

1. Lee Roy Yarborough (1969) and David Pearson (1976)
2. 25th
3. Darrell Waltrip
4. Winston
5. 175
6. 31
7. 5
8. Jeff Gordon
9. 150
10. Talladega
11. Dale Earnhardt
12. Brickyard
13. Fireball Roberts
14. David Pearson
15. Tommy Houston

Great American Stock Car Racing

FIRST AND LAST

1. Which driver won the first Brickyard 400?

2. He won his first race at New Hampshire after surviving a near fatal crash at Michigan in 1994.

3. She was the first woman driver in a Winston Cup race in the modern era. Name her.

4. Of her 31 races between 1976 and 1978, which was her first?

5. There were no first time Winston Cup winners in 1972. True or False?

6. Who was the first to win the Daytona 500 and the Brickyard 400 in the same year?

7. Who won the 1996 exhibition at Suzuka City, Japan?

8. Which NASCAR driver was the first to compete in Japan?

9. The first drivers inducted into the National Motorsports Press Association Stock Car Hall of Fame were Joe Weatherly, Herb Thomas, mechanic Paul McDuffie and this driver.

10. Who won the last Winston Cup race at North Wilkesboro?

11. Richard Petty made his first million in what year?

12. It took 74 hours to determine the first winner of the 1959 _____.

13. The first Daytona 500 was run caution free. True or false?

14. The first NMPS "Driver of the Year" was which Yarborough?

15. Which late Winston Cup driver won his first race in 1987?

FIRST AND LAST

ANSWERS

1. Jeff Gordon
2. Ernie Irvan
3. Janet Guthrie
4. World 600
5. True
6. Dale Jarrett
7. Rusty Wallace
8. Tiny Lund (1970 stock car race)
9. "Fireball" Roberts
10. Jeff Gordon
11. 1971
12. Daytona 500
13. True
14. Lee Roy
15. Davey Allison

Great American Stock Car Racing

WRECKS

1. Which Winston Cup driver "flew" out of the track at Talladega? He was later nicknamed "Air."

2. Three drivers' lives were taken in on-track wrecks in 1964: Joe Weatherly, Fireball Roberts and who?

3. Two wrecks at Talladega in April 1996 were dramatic, yet the drivers walked away. Name the main drivers involved.

4. Dale Earnhardt has seen two bad wrecks in his 18 year career, one in _____ and one in 1996.

5. This driver flipped at Talladega and which other track in 1993?

Great American Stock Car Racing

6. This driver saw his car virtually destroyed at Talladega in July 1995.

7. This BGN driver was fortunate to only have burned his hands and neck in a Homestead, Florida, explosion during a last chance race in 1996.

8. After this wreck during the 1979 Daytona 500, these three drivers stepped out of their car on the backstretch and proceeded to fight it out.

9. Sadly, these drivers have been killed as a result of the _____ qualifying races for the Daytona 500: Talmadge Prince (1970), Friday Hassler (1972), Ricky Knotts (1980), Bruce Jacobi (1987).

10. Michael Waltrip's totally destroyed car, involved in a wreck at _____, sits in the museum at Talladega.

11. This track has been the scene of more bizarre incidents than any other on the circuit.

12. Which racing legend saw his career end early due to a wreck at Pocono in 1988?

13. This champion miraculously survived a tumbling roll down the front straightaway at Daytona.

14. This driver captured a heart-stopping win over Richard Petty on the final lap after the two crashed in one of the most famous Daytona 500 races ever.

15. Cole Trickle T-boned what driver in *Days of Thunder*?

Great American Stock Car Racing

WRECKS

ANSWERS

1. Jimmy Horton
2. Jimmy Pardue
3. Ricky Craven and Bill Elliot
4. 1979
5. Daytona
6. Ken Schrader
7. Michael Laughlin
8. Donnie Allison, Bobby Allison and Cale Yarborough
9. Twin 125
10. Bristol
11. Talladega
12. Bobby Allison
13. Daytona
14. David Pearson
15. Rowdy Barnes

Great American Stock Car Racing

CRAFTSMAN TRUCK SERIES

1. Who was the first female driver in a truck race?

2. The first black man to race a truck was

   _____.

3. The series' first champion moved to Winston Cup in 1997. Name him.

4. This 1996 series champion took over for Ricky Craven after he was hurt at Talladega in 1996.

5. Three truck drivers went to Japan for the exhibition race. They were Mike Skinner, Ron Hornaday and _____.

6. The trucks moved to Orlando in 1997 to race at this "magical" speedway.

7. This man was the first winner of the series' Rookie of the Year award.

8. What corporation owns the truck driven by Ron Hornaday, Jr.?

9. The series is sponsored by this subsidiary of Sears.

10. The trucks were previewed in what series on TNN prior to their first season?

11. Who was the first winner of a truck race?

12. This retired Winston Cup driver resurfaced as a truck driver.

13. This 1992 Winston Cup Rookie of the Year now drives a truck.

14. Craftsman Truck Series drivers take a break halfway through the race. True or False?

15. The youngest truck competitor was just 16 when he raced for Bobby Hamilton at the Nashville, Tennessee, 1996 event. Name the young Hamilton protégé.

Great American Stock Car Racing

CRAFTSMAN TRUCK SERIES

ANSWERS

1. Tammy Jo Kirk
2. Felix Giles
3. Mike Skinner
4. Ron Hornaday, Jr.
5. Rick Carelli
6. Walt Disney World
7. Bryan Reffner
8. Dale Earnhardt, Inc.
9. Craftsman
10. Winter Heat
11. Mike Skinner
12. Harry Gant
13. Jimmy Hensley
14. True
15. Casey Atwood

Great American Stock Car Racing

DRIVERS

1. Which two drivers switched teams mid-year in 1996?

2. This Bodine first drove for Rick Hendrick.

3. This Winston Cup driver created bobsleds for the Olympic team.

4. What former driver for Bobby Allison Motorsports was the 1983 Late Model Sportsman Champion?

5. These two drivers shared the 1986 "Driver of the Year" award.

6. His 1988 championship made him the first Ford driver to win the title since David Pearson.

7. He was the youngest title holder since Bill Rexford won in 1950.

8. Who raced go-karts, CART, USAC, Le Mans, Indy, NHRA and more before moving to Winston Cup?

9. This driver won the 1993 Busch Grand National championship.

10. His big break came in the "Superstar Showdown" at Nashville in 1988. He beat Bill Elliot, Darrell Waltrip and others.

11. Who was 22 when he won the Talladega 500?

12. Despite his near fatal wreck, this driver won the 1994 True Value Hard Charger Award. He had competed in just 20 events that year.

Great American Stock Car Racing

13. Who is nearly a scratch handicap golfer?

14. His first career win came in the 1995 Coca Cola 600.

15. At Bristol in 1996, he clashed with Dale Earnhardt and came across the line backwards. His was one of the few cars in Victory Lane that was actually torn up!

Great American Stock Car Racing

DRIVERS

ANSWERS

1. Jeremy Mayfield and John Andretti
2. Brett
3. Geoff Bodine (the Bo-Dyn sled)
4. Derrike Cope
5. Dale Earnhardt and Tim Richmond
6. Bill Elliot
7. Jeff Gordon
8. John Andretti
9. Steve Grissom
10. Bobby Hamilton
11. Bobby Hillen
12. Ernie Irvan
13. Dale Jarrett
14. Bobby Labonte
15. Terry Labonte

MORE DRIVERS

1. This driver is known for his black leather hard-soled shoes he wears during the races.

2. This Tennessee native made his Winston Cup debut after his dad broke his shoulder in a 1976 crash.

3. Name the driver who won four races in a row in 1993.

4. Who won the pole for the first Brickyard 400?

5. This young driver grew up in Owensboro, Kentucky, idolizing Darrell Waltrip.

6. Name the man who co-hosts a Family Channel racing show with Ole D.W.

7. This 1990 BGN Rookie of the Year was the champion in 1992.

8. Who was the first third generation driver to win a Cup race?

9. This Asheville, North Carolina, driver replaced Harry Gant in the #33 car.

10. Although he has won at least one race each year since 1993, this driver has never won more than two in a year.

11. He and his wife Patty Moise both drive stock cars. Who is he?

12. This driver was the World Karting Champion, taking the title in Le Mans, France, in 1978.

13. Which driver filled in for Ernie Irvan after Irvan's crash in 1994?

14. Name the Penske driver who won the 1991 IROC.

15. This driver won a close rookie battle with Robert Pressley in 1995.

MORE DRIVERS

ANSWERS

1. Dave Marcis
2. Sterling Marlin
3. Mark Martin
4. Rick Mast
5. Jeremy Mayfield
6. Ted Musgrave
7. Joe Nemechek
8. Kyle Petty
9. Robert Pressley
10. Ricky Rudd
11. Elton Sawyer
12. Lake Speed
13. Kenny Wallace
14. Rusty Wallace
15. Ricky Craven

 **Great American Stock Car Racing**

TRUE OR FALSE, PART TWO

1. An Edsel ran in the first Daytona 500.

2. Both Derrick Cope and Jeff Gordon married former Miss Winstons.

3. ARCA is sanctioned by NASCAR.

4. A Chevy truck was the "pace car" for the second Brickyard 400.

5. Mario Andretti drove for Richard Petty in 1995.

6. Jeff Gordon won his first pole at Rockingham.

7. Brooks & Dunn and Rusty Wallace wrote the song "Sunday Money" together. The song was featured on a later album.

8. John Andretti is the only person to have wrecked cars in both Winston Cup and Indy car divisions at Indianapolis.

9. The Alan Kulwicki Park is located in Bristol.

10. "Tie Rod" is the official mascot of Charlotte Motor Speedway.

11. Randolph Scott was the first African-American NASCAR driver.

12. Junior Johnson spent a year in jail for bootlegging.

13. Motor Racing Outreach is the ministerial organization of NASCAR.

14. Harry Gant's Farewell Tour was in 1992.

15. A brick from the Brickyard was laid at Walt Disney World Speedway.

TRUE OR FALSE, PART TWO

ANSWERS

1. True
2. True
3. False
4. True
5. False, it was John Andretti.
6. False, it was at Charlotte.
7. False, Dale Earnhardt was the driver, and the album was the Dale Earnhardt Winston Cup Collection.
8. True
9. False, it is in Greenfield, Wisconsin.
10. False, it's name is "Lug Nut."
11. False, his name was Wendall Scott.
12. True
13. True
14. False, it was in 1994.
15. True

Great American Stock Car Racing

PART-TIME JOBS

1. This former Winston Cup driver owns a steakhouse in Taylor, North Carolina. He also used to be a carpenter.

2. What current star was a welder on the Charlotte Motor Speedway grandstands when he first moved to Charlotte?

3. This driver owns a Honda dealership in Franklin, Tennessee.

4. Which driver once had a country music "career" as well as a driving career?

5. This driver worked on his older brother Benny's Winston Cup team before getting his own rides.

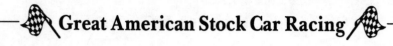

6. This driver has raced just about everything. He still finds time to co-own auto parts stores.

7. He is a former volunteer fireman.

8. Which driver enjoys working as a TV announcer when he's not driving or rooting for the St. Louis Cardinals?

9. This driver could take an automobile apart and put it back together when he was 11.

10. He spends his "off time" racing at small tracks in the Midwest (when he's not running his own dirt track).

11. Who was a professional baseball prospect (as a catcher) before a knee injury ended his career?

12. This independent driver would like to run a fishing resort or restaurant when his driving days are through.

13. Who teamed up with Cleveland Cavaliers center Brad Daugherty to form his BGN team?

14. This country music artist's part-time career was Grand National racing. He competed in 43 races during his career.

15. This driver (later car owner) ran moonshine for his family when he first broke into racing.

Great American Stock Car Racing

PART-TIME JOBS

ANSWERS

1. Harry Gant
2. Ernie Irvan
3. Darrell Waltrip
4. Kyle Petty
5. Phil Parsons
6. John Andretti
7. Geoff Bodine
8. Kenny Wallace
9. Morgan Shepherd
10. Kenny Schrader
11. Derrike Cope
12. Dave Marcis
13. Robert Pressley
14. Marty Robbins
15. Junior Johnson

Great American Stock Car Racing

THE LEGENDS

1. Which legendary car owner and crew chief won the 1962 and 1963 Winston Cup championships with Joe Weatherly as driver?

2. After this driver won the 1956 championship, he took over the ownership of his team. He won again. Now there's a driving school in his name.

3. This "Golden Boy of the 60's" was the first driver to top $100,000 in a single season. He was also the first to score a Grand Slam with victories on the original five superspeedways.

4. This current flagman used to work in the same position at Nashville Speedway. He worked with drivers such as Darrell Waltrip, Jimmy Means and Sterling Marlin.

5. Which Grand National driver is a former movie stuntman, working on films such as "Speedway" and "Six Pack"?

6. This younger brother of The King is a master engine builder.

7. Who was the first Miss Winston, starting in the 1971 season?

8. Second only to Richard Petty on the all-time list of wins and poles, this former driver set innumerable records during his 26 year career.

9. This late driver was Winston Cup's pace car driver when he died during a tour of the Suzuka City Circuitland track in 1996.

10. Who won the 1975 Daytona 500 and now works as a color commentator on television coverage of Winston Cup races?

11. This father of a current Winston Cup driver now owns a tobacco farm near Columbia, Tennessee.

12. This legendary driver is one of the original members of the Alabama Gang.

13. Which late flagman had the duty for more than 25 years before retiring after the May 6 Talladega race in 1990?

14. Born in Chicago, this driver went on to win five poles and two races. He's known for his innovations, including the NASCAR screw jack, first used in 1955.

15. This driver won the 1961 and 1965 championships while gaining a name for himself as one of
the most personable drivers on the circuit. Today,
one son has joined him in the television world
while the other son races.

Great American Stock Car Racing

THE LEGENDS

ANSWERS

1. Walter "Bud" Moore
2. Buck Baker
3. Fred Lorenzen
4. Doyle Ford
5. Neil "Soapy" Castles
6. Maurice Petty
7. Marilyn Green
8. David Pearson
9. Elmo Langley
10. Benny Parsons
11. Clifton "Coo Coo" Marlin
12. Bobby Allison
13. Harold Kinder
14. "Tiger" Tom Pistone
15. Ned Jarrett

If your local bookstore or souvenir shop is out of **GREAT AMERICAN STOCK CAR RACING**, and you'd like to have a couple extra copies for the guys in the pit, you can order direct by sending a check or money order made payable to PREMIUM PRESS AMERICA for $8.95 ($6.95 plus $2.00 shipping).

GREAT AMERICAN STOCK CAR RACING
PREMIUM PRESS AMERICA
P.O. Box 159015
Nashville, TN 37215-9015
(800) 891-7323
(615) 256-8484

Other Premium Press America Stock Car books:

STOCK CAR TRIVIA ENCYCLOPEDIA: The ABC's of Racing!
STOCK CAR FUN & GAMES: Puzzles, Word Games, and More!
STOCK CAR LEGENDS: The Laughs, Practical Jokes, and Fun Stories from
   Racing's Greats!
STOCK CAR DRIVERS & TRACKS: Featuring NASCAR's Greatest Drivers!

A companion book to **GREAT AMERICAN STOCK CAR RACING** is also available: **GREAT AMERICAN COUNTRY MUSIC.** For multiple copies and/or more than one title send:

2 books: $11.95 plus $2.00 shipping=$13.95
3 books: $15.95 plus $2.00 shipping=$17.95
4 books: $18.95 plus $2.00 shipping=$20.95

Allow 2-4 weeks for delivery.